D0753529

Quick Gourmet Dishes

by Sheryl Julian

BARRON'S
Woodbury, New York · London · Toronto · Sydney

© Copyright 1984 by Barron's Educational
Series, Inc.

All inquiries should be addressed to:

Barron's Educational Series, Inc.
113 Crossways Park Drive
Woodbury, New York 11797

International Standard Book
No. 0-8120-5558-6
Library of Congress Catalog Card
No. 83-22439

**Library of Congress Cataloging
in Publication Data**
Julian, Sheryl.
  Quick gourmet dishes.

  (Easy cooking)
  Includes index.
  1. Cookery. I. Title. II. Series.
TX652.J85 1984   641.5   83-22439
ISBN 0-8120-5558-6

PRINTED IN HONG KONG
  4 5 6   490   9 8 7 6 5 4 3 2 1

Credits

Photography
Color photographs: Irwin Horowitz
Food stylist: Helen Feingold
Stylist: Hal Walter

Author Sheryl Julian is the contributing
food writer and stylist for the *Boston Globe
Magazine*. She trained at the Cordon Bleu
Schools in London and Paris.

Cover and book design Milton Glaser,
Inc.

Series editor Carole Berglie

INTRODUCTION

Most cooking teachers agree that there are three essentials to producing meals quickly every night: mastery of basic skills like chopping, so small tasks don't impede the preparation process; ready availability of several of the basic ingredients found in most recipes, fully prepared and waiting to be added to a dish; and a repertoire of dishes with which the cook is comfortable.

While it is true that cooking is easier for some people than for others, there are some things that even the very good cooks in the world cannot avoid. Everyone must shop for food, bring it home, and unpack it—all before any cooking begins. What becomes exhausting is having to do all these chores just before the cooking, so the process is far longer than it should be and so tiring that a recipe labeled "quick" feels like a joke.

The ordinary skills any cook needs to make preparations more efficient are rarely emphasized. Chopping an onion should be so routine that it is accomplished without thinking. The cook who runs to the food processor to chop one onion loses out later: the processor needs to be washed (or dishwashed) and then put away.

To shorten the preparation time, there are some standard ingredients that can be assembled and refrigerated: chopped onions, chopped peppers, and chopped parsley, for instance, can be stored in tightly covered jars; crushed or finely chopped garlic will keep well in a small jar of olive oil (and give the oil pungency); chopped shallots left in wine (white or red) will lend it a distinctive taste that benefits the finished dish. A week's chopped onions, peppers, parsley, garlic, and shallots will take a short time to do all at once and speed you up considerably when it is time to cook.

In addition to the ingredients you will need during the week, you can also prepare salads and vegetables. Salad greens will live well in a plastic bag after washing; most vegetables do not suffer if they are cut up a day or two beforehand and covered tightly; all grains reheat perfectly if transferred to a buttered casserole and warmed in a moderate oven.

For nightly meals, dinner should be the simpler and more familiar dishes. Try new dishes on the weekends but make the reliable ones at the end of a hectic day. When guests are expected, venture into dishes you've been meaning to try. But make sure that at least some part of your company meal is already waiting in the fridge: a first-course salad, a soup ready for reheating, a chilled dessert. In recent years, the enthusiasm for lavish dinner parties—where the food was in some stage of preparation for half the day—left some of the host's responsibilities neglected. What fun is it, after all, to come to someone's house for dinner and find that the cook has so much work left to do that he or she disappears after an initial greeting? It can be terribly uncomfortable for guests to be left alone while the host is off in the kitchen, so any experimenting with new dishes should not be too ambitious.

The recipes in this book represent a range of light supper dishes and dinner-party suggestions that require only elementary skills and widely available ingredients. They include such popular restaurant offerings as smoked fish pâté or rack of lamb with tiny potatoes; food that can be found in the fancy carryouts, such as tortellini salad or poached chicken with red-pepper sauce; and versions of dishes that you might have sampled for years, including fillet steaks with Bearnaise sauce and apricot bread pudding. They all are designed to make your stay in the kitchen brief while the food you present garners ovations. Happy cooking.

UNDERSTANDING THE RECIPE ANALYSES

For each recipe in this book, you'll note that we have provided data on the quantities of protein, fat, sodium, carbohydrates, and potassium, as well as the number of calories (kcal) per serving. If you are on a low-calorie diet or are watching your intake of sodium, for example, these figures should help you gauge your eating habits and help you balance your meals. Bear in mind, however, that the calculations are fundamentally estimates and are to be followed only in a very general way. The actual quantity of fat, for example, that may be contained in a given portion will vary with the quality of meat you buy or with how much care you take in skimming off cooking fat. If you are on a rigid diet, consult your physician. The analyses are based on the number of portions given as the yield for the recipe, but if the yield reads, "4 to 6 servings," we indicate which number of servings (4, for example) was used to determine the final amounts.

MENU SUGGESTIONS

NOTE: Recipes included in this book are preceded by ●.

- ● Dilled salmon terrine
  Broiled baby chickens
- ● Strawberry fool

- ● Cream of carrot soup
- ● Rack of lamb with tiny potatoes
  Pecan ice cream with crisp cookies

- ● Roasted red pepper salad
  Fettuccine with white clam sauce
- ● Thin apple tart

- ● Goat cheese soufflé
- ● Roast lamb with eggplant
  Poached pears

- ● Tortellini and ham salad
  Roast capon
  Chocolate cake

- ● Shredded vegetable and pasta soup
  Spinach salad
  Garlic bread
  Gingerbread with whipped cream

- ● Smoked fish pâté
  Loin of pork
  Lemon pound cake

- ● Fettuccine with blue cheese sauce
- ● Chicken in parchment paper
- ● Sautéed apples with vanilla custard sauce

- ● Seviche of scallops
  Broiled lamb chops
- ● Apricot bread pudding

  Cream of spinach soup
- ● Cornish hens with rosemary
- ● Cherry tomato and basil sauté
  Lemon tart

- ● Asparagus or broccoli mimosa
- ● Poached haddock in tomato sauce
  Fresh pineapple with macaroons

  Fresh noodles in garlic and cream
- ● Ragout of chicken legs
- ● Orange creams

- ● Herbed salmon steaks
- ● Julienne vegetable sauté
  Lemon sherbet with lace cookies

  Caesar salad
- ● Poached chicken with red pepper sauce
  Rice pilaf
  Melon wedges with lime

  Mussels steamed in white wine
- ● Braised pork chops with apples
  Broiled rice
- ● Raspberries Romanoff

- ● Fillet steaks with mock Bearnaise
- ● Italian steamed vegetables
  Fresh strawberries and cream

- ● Thatched potatoes in cream
  Roast beef
  Broiled tomatoes
  Sliced oranges with Grand Marnier

- ● Saffron fish chowder
  Buttered pumpernickel toast
  Sliced tomato salad
  Pound cake with coffee ice cream & fudge sauce

- ● Corn, ham and potato chowder
  Hot cornbread
  Boston lettuce salad
  Hermits or gingersnaps

YIELD

Serves 6

Per serving
calories 405, protein 28 g,
fat 13 g, sodium 190 mg,
carbohydrates 2 g,
potassium 617 mg

TIME

15 minutes preparation
2 hours chilling
30 minutes cooking

INGREDIENTS

1½ pounds boneless skinless salmon
1 egg + 1 extra white
Salt and freshly ground black pepper
    to taste
Squeeze of lemon juice
1 cup heavy cream
Large handful fresh dill sprigs, finely
    chopped
Boston or bibb lettuce for serving

Set the oven at 325 degrees.

Cut the salmon into small pieces and work them with the egg and extra white in a food processor until they are quite smooth. Add salt, pepper, and lemon juice and process just to combine. Pour the heavy cream through the feed tube and process to mix thoroughly, but turn off the machine as soon as the cream is incorporated. Transfer the mixture to a bowl, stir in the dill (reserving a few sprigs for garnish) and set aside.

Butter a 1-quart loaf pan and line the bottom and sides with foil cut to fit it ①. Butter the foil and spoon the fish mixture into the pan, pressing it down well ②. Bang the pan on the counter to settle any air pockets and cut a piece of foil to seal the top. Butter it and press it buttered side down onto the terrine.

Set the loaf pan in a roasting pan and pour enough boiling water to come halfway up the sides of the loaf pan ③. Bake the terrine for 30 minutes or until the fish feels firm when pressed on the top with a fingertip.

Remove the loaf pan from the water and let it cool off slightly. Refrigerate for 2 hours or until cold.

To serve, line 6 salad plates with some lettuce. Cut the terrine into thick slices and arrange 1 on each plate. Garnish the slice with some reserved dill sprigs and serve at once as an appetizer with buttered toast.

2

YIELD

Serves 6

Per serving
calories 278, protein 6 g,
fat 21 g, sodium 859 mg,
carbohydrates 14 g,
potassium 521 mg

TIME

10 minutes preparation
20 minutes cooking

INGREDIENTS

3 tablespoons butter
6 medium carrots, thinly sliced
1 onion, chopped
3 tablespoons flour
Salt and freshly ground black pepper
    to taste
Pinch of sugar
5 cups chicken stock
1 cup heavy cream, softly whipped
3 tablespoons snipped fresh chives for
    garnish

Melt the butter in a large saucepan and cook the carrots and onion over a medium-low heat for 5 minutes. Stir in the flour and cook, stirring, for 2 minutes ①. Add salt, pepper, sugar, and chicken stock; turn up the heat and let the mixture come to a boil, stirring constantly ②. Lower the heat, cover the pan, and let the soup simmer, stirring occasionally, for 15 minutes or until the carrots are tender.

Purée the soup in a blender or food processor ③ and pour it back into the pan. Bring to a boil, taste for seasoning, and ladle into bowls. Garnish each bowl with a spoonful of whipped cream and top the cream with some chives. Serve at once.

YIELD

Serves 4

Per serving
calories 322, protein 2g,
fat 30 g, sodium 158 mg,
carbohydrates 13 g,
potassium 407 mg

TIME

10 minutes preparation
30 minutes chilling
15 minutes cooking

INGREDIENTS

6 large red bell peppers
½ cup top-quality olive oil
2 shallots, very finely chopped
Salt and freshly ground black pepper
    to taste
¼ cup imported black olives

Preheat the broiler. Set the peppers in a small roasting pan and rub them very lightly with olive oil, reserving the remaining oil for later. Broil the peppers as close to the element as possible, turning them every few minutes or as soon as they are charred on one side ①. When they are charred all over—this may take 15 minutes altogether—drop them into a large bowl of ice water and leave for a few minutes or until they are cold.

Remove the peppers from the water and work over a bowl to cut off the stem end, split each lengthwise in half, and discard the ribs and seeds ②. Peel off the charred skins ③ and arrange 3 halves on each of 4 salad plates.

Sprinkle the remaining oil on the peppers and decorate each plate with a thin band of chopped shallots running across the peppers. Wrap tightly and refrigerate 15 to 30 minutes or until cold.

Just before serving, sprinkle with salt and pepper and garnish each plate with black olives. Serve as an appetizer with thick slices of toasted Italian bread and butter.

YIELD

Serves 4

Per serving
calories 390, protein 12 g,
fat 27 g, sodium 481 mg,
carbohydrates 22 g,
potassium 186 mg

TIME

15 minutes preparation
35 minutes cooking

INGREDIENTS

4 tablespoons butter
3 tablespoons browned bread crumbs
2 tablespoons flour
1 cup milk
¼ pound dry goat cheese, such as
    Bucheron or Pouligny
1 heaping teaspoon Dijon-style
    mustard
Pinch of cayenne
Freshly ground black pepper to taste
4 eggs, separated
1 extra egg white

Set the oven at 400 degrees. Use 1 tablespoon of the butter to grease an 8-cup soufflé dish. Use half the bread crumbs to coat the inside of the dish ①.

Melt the remaining butter in a saucepan and whisk in the flour. Add the milk off the heat, whisking constantly until the mixture is completely smooth, then return to the heat and cook, stirring constantly, until it comes to a boil. Simmer gently for 2 minutes, then remove from the heat. Crumble the goat cheese and add it to the hot sauce (remove any rind on the cheese). Add the mustard, cayenne, black pepper, and egg yolks, 1 at a time.

Beat the 5 egg whites until they hold stiff peaks ② and stir 1 large spoonful into the hot sauce. Fold in the remaining whites as lightly as possible ③, then pour the soufflé mixture into the dish. Sprinkle the remaining bread crumbs on top and bake the soufflé for 35 minutes or until it is puffed and brown and set in the middle. Quickly tie a white linen napkin around the collar of the dish and set in on a platter. Serve at once with a large spoon.

YIELD

Serves 4

Per serving
calories 993, protein 28 g,
fat 83 g, sodium 1085 mg,
carbohydrates 33 g,
potassium 524 mg

TIME

25 minutes preparation
1 hour chilling
5 minutes cooking

INGREDIENTS

⅓ cup white wine vinegar
1 teaspoon egg yolk
1 teaspoon Dijon-style mustard
Pinch of cayenne
1 cup olive oil
Salt and freshly ground black pepper
   to taste
1 pound fresh or frozen cheese-filled
   tortellini

½ pound Black Forest, Virginia, or
   other flavorful ham, cut in 2 thick
   slices
2 stalks broccoli
2 tablespoons peanut oil

In a blender combine the vinegar, egg yolk, mustard, and cayenne. Whirl at high speed, then leave the motor on and add the oil through the insert in the cap, pouring it in a thin, steady stream ①. Add plenty of salt and pepper to taste and set aside.

Bring a large saucepan of water to the boil, add the tortellini, and cook about 2 minutes or until they are tender. Drain and shake well to remove excess moisture. Pile into a bowl and pour in the dressing from the blender.

Cut the ham into matchstick pieces ② and add to the tortellini.

Cut the broccoli stems from the stalks (use the stalks for another dish) and make the flowerets as tiny as possible ③. Heat the peanut oil in a large skillet and sauté the broccoli over a high heat for 2 minutes. Add 2 tablespoons water, cover, and steam over high heat for another minute. Lift the broccoli from the pan and let it cool to lukewarm on a plate. Add to the tortellini and stir thoroughly. Cover and chill 1 hour, then taste for seasoning and serve.

YIELD

Serves 4

Per serving
calories 425, protein 23 g,
fat 25 g, sodium 1545 mg,
carbohydrates 25 g,
potassium 792 mg

TIME

10 minutes preparation
15 minutes cooking

INGREDIENTS

3 scallions, trimmed at both ends
3 medium zucchini
3 medium carrots
4 tablespoons butter
1/4 pound baked ham, thickly sliced
4 cups chicken stock
1/3 cup orzo pasta or 3/4 cup fusilli
    (corkscrew) pasta
1 cup freshly grated parmesan cheese
    for serving

Slice the scallions and set aside ①. Shred the zucchini and carrots ②. Melt the butter in a large saucepan and cook the scallions for 3 minutes over a low heat. Add the zucchini and carrots ③ and continue cooking 5 minutes, stirring once or twice, until the zucchini begin to release their liquid.

Cut the ham into matchstick pieces and add to the vegetables with the chicken stock. Bring to a boil, cover, and simmer gently for 5 minutes.

Meanwhile, cook the orzo or fusilli in plenty of boiling salted water for 4 minutes for the orzo or 8 minutes for the fusilli or until tender. Drain and add to the soup. Reheat to boiling and serve sprinkled with parmesan cheese. Pass garlic bread separately.

YIELD

Serves 6

Per serving
calories 153, protein 4 g,
fat 15 g, sodium 1179 mg,
potassium 34 mg

TIME

15 minutes preparation
1 hour chilling

INGREDIENTS

2 smoked trout (whole or boned) or
  2 smoked mackerel
½ cup unsalted butter, at room
  temperature
Freshly ground black pepper to taste
1 large sprig flat leaf parsley for
  decoration

If necessary, skin the trout or mackerel ①, discarding the heads and tails. Pull the flesh from the bones ② and run your fingers down the fillets to feel for any of the tiny bones hiding there. Pile the boned fillets into a food processor or blender and work them with the butter and black pepper until completely smooth.

Pack the pâté into a 3-cup crock or bowl and smooth the top with a metal palette knife. "Pleat" the top with a small palette knife so the surface looks like a bicycle wheel ③. Cover with plastic wrap and chill 1 hour.

Just before serving, let the pâté sit out for 10 minutes to soften slightly, then tuck the parsley sprig into the center of the pâté and pass triangles of dry toast separately.

YIELD

Serves 4

Per serving
calories 1291, protein 46 g,
fat 64 g, sodium 1456 mg,
carbohydrates 130 g,
potassium 550 mg

TIME

5 minutes preparation
5 minutes cooking

INGREDIENTS

1½ cups heavy cream
Freshly ground black pepper to taste
½ pound Roquefort, stilton or danish
   blue cheese, crumbled
2 cups broccoli flowerets
1½ pounds fresh fettuccine noodles
1 cup freshly grated parmesan cheese
   for serving

Bring a large stockpot of water to the boil for cooking the fettuccine.

Meanwhile in a heavy-based saucepan, combine the cream, pepper, and crumbled blue cheese and set over a low heat. Leave the sauce to heat gently, stirring occasionally, until it just reaches the boiling point.

Cut the broccoli flowerets into the smallest possible pieces ① and drop them into a saucepan of rapidly boiling water (not the water for cooking the fettuccine) ②. Cook 1 minute or until they are just done and still slightly crunchy, then drain ③ and set aside.

Cook the fettuccine in the rapidly boiling stockpot of water just until the noodles rise to the surface, about 2 minutes, or until they are tender but still have some bite.

Drain at once, shaking them in the colander, then divide the noodles among 4 dinner plates. Scatter some broccoli on each serving and divide the sauce among them. Serve at once, passing parmesan cheese separately.

SEVICHE OF SCALLOPS

YIELD

Serves 4

Per serving
calories 138, protein 22 g,
sodium 436 mg,
carbohydrates 10 g,
potassium 763 mg

TIME

15 minutes preparation
2 hours chilling

INGREDIENTS

1 1/4 pounds fresh scallops
Juice of 2 limes
2 dried or fresh hot peppers
Slice of red onion
2 tomatoes, dipped for 10 seconds
  into boiling water
Salt to taste
4 leaves of leaf lettuce for serving

Pile the scallops into a bowl and sprinkle the lime juice onto them. Halve the dried peppers, shake out the seeds ①, and chop the flesh. (Wear rubber gloves to seed and chop the fresh peppers.) Add peppers to the scallops and cover tightly. Refrigerate for 2 hours (up to 5 hours), turning gently every half hour.

Cut the onion slice into 1/2-inch lengths and add to the scallops.

Peel the tomatoes, discarding the cores ②. Halve them horizontally and squeeze each half to remove the seeds ③. Cut the flesh into strips and add to the scallops with salt to taste. Stir gently, then serve on lettuce, lifting each portion from the marinade with a slotted spoon.

YIELD

Serves 6

Per serving
calories 501, protein 53 g,
fat 29 g, sodium 236 mg,
carbohydrates 1 g,
potassium 462 mg

TIME

20 minutes preparation
40 minutes cooking

INGREDIENTS

6 Cornish hens, thawed if necessary
Salt and freshly ground black pepper
    to taste
About ½ cup sour cream
2 teaspoons dried rosemary

Set the oven at 425 degrees.

Take the giblets from the hens and reserve them for another use. Pull out the pockets of fat at the opening and set the birds breast side down on a board. Use poultry shears to cut up either side of the backbone on each bird, lifting out and discarding them ①. Separate the 2 cut sides so the hens are almost flat. Turn them over and press firmly with the heel of your hand right in the center of the breastbone so the hens lie completely flat ②. Tuck the wing pinions back to expose the breasts and bend up the "knees" of the hens so they are even on both sides ③.

Put the hens into a large roasting pan skin side up and sprinkle them with salt and pepper. Rub some of the sour cream onto each bird. Crush the rosemary in the palm of your hand and sprinkle some rosemary onto each one.

Bake the hens in the preheated oven for 40 minutes or until they are golden brown on top and cooked through. Transfer each to a dinner plate and serve with sautéed snow peas.

YIELD

Serves 4

Per serving
calories 84, protein 1 g,
fat 7 g, sodium 72 mg,
carbohydrates 4 g,
potassium 223 mg

TIME

5 minutes preparation
3 minutes cooking

INGREDIENTS

1½ pints cherry tomatoes, stems
     removed
2 tablespoons olive oil
2 cloves garlic, crushed
2 shallots, very finely chopped ①
Handful of fresh basil leaves, finely
     chopped ②
Salt and freshly ground black pepper
     to taste
Extra basil leaves for garnish

Have the cherry tomatoes sitting near the stove. Heat the olive oil in a large skillet and when it is quite hot, add the cherry tomatoes, garlic, and shallots. Cook over a medium-high heat, shaking the pan constantly ③, for 1 to 3 minutes or until the cherry tomatoes are tender but have not shriveled or burst.

Remove them from the pan and transfer to a serving dish. Sprinkle with basil, salt, and pepper and stir well to combine them. Garnish with extra basil leaves and serve at once.

YIELD

Serves 4

Per serving
calories 389, protein 44 g,
fat 14 g, sodium 382 mg,
carbohydrates 14 g,
potassium 1197 mg

TIME

10 minutes preparation
15 minutes cooking

INGREDIENTS

4 haddock steaks or fillets, each ½
   pound (or use cod or perch)
¼ cup olive oil
2 onions, chopped
2 medium carrots, thinly sliced
1 can (1 pound) Italian-style plum
   tomatoes
1 clove garlic, crushed
½ cup white wine

Salt and freshly ground black pepper
   to taste
Small handful of fresh parsley sprigs,
   finely chopped

Leave the fish at room temperature while you prepare the sauce.

Heat the oil in a large skillet that has a tight-fitting lid. Cook the onions over a low heat for 2 minutes or until they are soft but not brown ①. Add the carrots, cover the pan, and continue cooking 2 minutes, stirring occasionally.

Crush the tomatoes in your hand as they are added to the pan ② and add the garlic, wine, and plenty of salt and pepper to taste. Bring to a boil and leave this sauce to bubble gently for 3 minutes, uncovered.

Set the fish into the sauce and spoon some of it on top ③. Turn the heat up so the liquid comes to a boil, then lower it, cover the pan, and let the fish cook gently for 10 minutes or until it is firm to the touch and white in color.

Serve in deep plates, sprinkling each portion with chopped parsley. Pass rice pilaf or small boiled potatoes separately.

YIELD

Serves 2

Per serving
calories 701, protein 51 g,
fat 37 g, sodium 242 mg,
carbohydrates 38 g,
potassium 1436 mg

TIME

30 minutes preparation
30 minutes cooking

INGREDIENTS

1 rack of baby lamb, trimmed of all
    its fat
1 tablespoon butter, at room
    temperature
Salt and freshly ground black pepper
    to taste
3 large all-purpose potatoes
2 tablespoons peanut oil
Bunch of watercress for garnish

Set the rack of lamb on a broiler pan and rub the fat side with butter. Sprinkle with salt and pepper and wrap the exposed bones with foil ①. Set aside for 10 minutes. Preheat the broiler.

Peel the potatoes and use a melon baller to scoop out rounds, cutting them as close together as possible to avoid wasting too much potato ②. (Cut up and use the scraps for making hash-browns.) Pile the balls into a saucepan and add cold water to cover. Bring to a boil and cook 1 minute. Drain and set aside until the lamb is half cooked.

Broil the lamb for 8 minutes on a side, setting it as close to the element as possible. This will give medium-rare lamb. Remove from the oven and let it sit in a warm place for 5 minutes more. (For medium-done lamb, broil it 11 minutes on a side; for well-done lamb, broil it 14 minutes on a side; in any case, let the meat rest after cooking for 5 minutes.)

Meanwhile, heat the peanut oil until it is quite hot, add the potatoes, and sauté them over a high heat ③, shaking the pan often, for 8 to 10 minutes or until they are tender and brown. Sprinkle with salt and pepper.

Carve the lamb and arrange 4 slices on each of 2 plates, crossing the exposed bones like swords. Arrange the potatoes on the plate and garnish with the watercress.

YIELD

Serves 6

Per serving
(for asparagus)
calories 163, protein 4 g,
fat 13 g, sodium 108 mg,
carbohydrates 8 g,
potassium 435 mg

TIME

15 minutes preparation
30 minutes chilling
12 minutes cooking

INGREDIENTS

2 pounds fresh asparagus or 1 large
  head fresh broccoli
2 tablespoons white or red wine
  vinegar
1 teaspoon Dijon-style mustard
Salt and freshly ground black pepper
  to taste
Pinch of cayenne
⅓ cup olive oil
1 egg

Break off the asparagus ends where they snap naturally when you bend the spears ①. Trim the ends of the broccoli and use a small paring knife to peel the tough strings from each broccoli stem ②. Cut each stem into thin stalks ③. Cook either asparagus or broccoli in a skillet of boiling water for about 3 minutes for the asparagus and 5 minutes for the broccoli, or until they are both just done but still quite green. Drain into a roasting pan and fill the pan with very cold water and ice. Leave the vegetables to cool, then lift them from the water, arrange on a platter, blot dry with a clean towel, and cover tightly with plastic wrap.

Whisk the vinegar, mustard, salt, pepper, and cayenne together. Gradually whisk in the oil in a thin steady stream until the dressing emulsifies. Cover and set aside.

Prick a hole in the rounded end of the egg and gradually lower it into a pan of boiling water. When the water returns to the boil let the egg cook steadily for 12 minutes. Drain and plunge into a bowl of very cold water. When cool, peel and halve. Separate the yolk from the white.

To serve, pour the dressing over the vegetables on the platter and work the egg white through a sieve to make a band across the stems. Use the same sieve to work the yolk through, making a thinner band next to the white one. Serve at once.

YIELD

Serves 4

Per serving
calories 708, protein 59 g,
fat 42 g, sodium 458 mg,
carbohydrates 6 g,
potassium 603 mg

TIME

15 minutes preparation
20 minutes cooking

INGREDIENTS

4 even-sized chicken legs
 (with thighs)
1 tablespoon oil
3 tablespoons butter
2 tablespoons flour
1/2 cup chicken stock
1 cup dry red wine
1 clove garlic, crushed
1 shallot, finely chopped
1 bay leaf

Salt and freshly ground black pepper
 to taste
2 tablespoons madeira wine
Bunch of watercress for garnish

Let the chicken legs sit at room temperature for 20 minutes. Heat the oil in a large skillet and add the butter. When the butter melts, brown the chicken legs a few at a time over a medium-high heat until they are all browned. Remove them from the pan and sprinkle in the flour ①. Cook, stirring, for 4 minutes, then pour in the chicken stock, wine, garlic, shallot, bay leaf, salt, pepper, and madeira ②. Bring the liquids to a boil, then replace the chicken legs skin side down ③ and cover the pan. Let the liquids return to the boil, then lower the heat and let the chicken simmer gently for 15 minutes or until the legs are cooked through.

Transfer the chicken legs to a platter and cover with foil; keep warm. Let the sauce return to a rolling boil and let it bubble vigorously until it is reduced by half. Remove the bay leaf and spoon the sauce over the chicken legs. Garnish with the watercress and serve at once.

NOTE The protruding knobs at the knuckle and thigh ends of the legs can be cut off with half-hole poultry shears.

ROAST LAMB WITH EGGPLANT

YIELD

Serves 4

Per serving
calories 911, protein 86 g,
fat 48 g, sodium 375 mg,
carbohydrates 32 g,
potassium 2088 mg

TIME

30 minutes preparation
45 minutes cooking

INGREDIENTS

5 pounds sirloin half of a leg of lamb,
*   boned at the market*
½ cup olive oil
1 tablespoon dried rosemary
Salt and freshly ground black pepper
*   to taste*
2 cloves garlic, cut in slivers
2 large eggplant, cut in large cubes
2 large onions, thinly sliced
3 green peppers, cut in strips

1 tablespoon tomato paste
¼ cup chicken stock
1 pint cherry tomatoes, stems
*   removed*
Handful of parsley sprigs, finely
*   chopped*

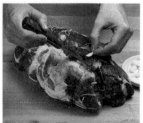

Set the oven at 425 degrees. Tie the meat several times so it stays compact. Rub the fat side with 1 tablespoon of the olive oil and sprinkle it with rosemary, salt, and pepper. Insert the garlic slivers all over the meat ① and set it in a roasting pan. Roast the meat for 45 minutes for rare lamb, 55 minutes for medium and 65 minutes for well done. Rare lamb registers 130 degrees on a meat thermometer; medium registers 140 degrees; well done registers 160 degrees.

Meanwhile, sprinkle salt over the eggplant ② and set it in a colander placed over a deep plate ③. Let it sit for 15 minutes, then rinse and dry with a clean kitchen towel.

Heat 3 tablespoons of the remaining oil in a large skillet and add the eggplant. Stir constantly over a high heat until there is no more oil in the bottom of the pan. Remove the eggplant. Add the remaining ¼ cup oil and cook the onions over a low heat until they are soft but not brown. Add the peppers with the tomato paste and stock and return the eggplant to the pan. Cover and cook over a medium-high heat for 20 minutes, stirring once or twice, until the eggplant is tender. Add black pepper to taste and stir in the cherry tomatoes.

Remove the strings from the lamb and carve it into thick slices. Arrange these on a platter and spoon the eggplant garnish beside it. Sprinkle the eggplant with parsley and serve at once.

YIELD

Serves 6

Per serving
calories 148, protein 2 g,
fat 12 g, sodium 86 mg,
carbohydrates 10 g,
potassium 415 mg

TIME

30 minutes preparation
6 minutes cooking

INGREDIENTS

2 medium carrots
2 zucchini
2 yellow squash
2 red bell peppers, cored and seeded
5 tablespoons olive oil
Salt and freshly ground black pepper
  to taste
Handful of fresh mint leaves, finely
  chopped
Handful of fresh parsley sprigs, finely
  chopped

Halve the carrots lengthwise and cut each half on an extreme diagonal to make matchsticks ①. Put them into a saucepan with cold water to cover, bring to a boil, and cook steadily for 2 minutes. Drain and rinse with cold water; set aside.

Cut a thin lengthwise slice from each zucchini, then cut another lengthwise slice from the same side ②. Turn the zucchini on its flat side and cut 2 more lengthwise slices from another long side ③. Continue in this fashion with the third and fourth sides, until there is only a column of seeds left. (Add these seeds to soups.) Cut the slices on an extreme diagonal to make matchstick shapes. Cut the yellow squash in the same way.

Cut the red peppers into strips of the same size.

Heat the olive oil in a large skillet and add the zucchini, squash, and carrots. Cook over a medium-high heat, stirring often, for 3 minutes or until they are slightly softened. Add the red pepper strips and continue cooking for another 3 minutes or until all the vegetables are tender but still have some bite.

Add salt, pepper, mint, and parsley; stir to mix, and serve at once with broiled or grilled meats or fish.

HERBED SALMON STEAKS

YIELD

Serves 6

Per serving
calories 537, protein 46 g,
fat 34 g, sodium 283 mg,
carbohydrates 7 g,
potassium 885 mg

TIME

10 minutes preparation
25 minutes cooking

INGREDIENTS

¼ cup unsalted butter, at room
    temperature
2 shallots, finely chopped
Handful of fresh chives, finely snipped
Handful of fresh parsley sprigs, finely
    chopped
Salt and freshly ground black pepper
    to taste
6 salmon steaks, each ½ pound
½ cup dry white bread crumbs

Set the oven at 400 degrees. Use 1 tablespoon of the butter to grease a large shallow baking dish. Combine the remaining butter in a small bowl with the shallots, chives, parsley, and plenty of salt and pepper to taste.

Set the salmon in the baking dish ① and spread some of the herb mixture on each one ②. Sprinkle them with the bread crumbs ③ and bake in the preheated oven for 25 minutes or until the salmon is cooked through and the bread crumbs are golden. If necessary, slide the dish under the broiler for 1 minute to brown the bread crumbs. Serve at once with sautéed potatoes.

YIELD

Serves 6

Per serving
calories 426, protein 33 g,
fat 28 g, sodium 192 mg,
carbohydrates 3 g,
potassium 357 mg

TIME

30 minutes preparation
10 minutes cooking

INGREDIENTS

3 large whole boneless chicken breasts
1½ tablespoons butter
¾ cup white wine
1 cup heavy cream
1 tablespoon olive oil
1 red bell pepper, cut in thin strips
Salt and freshly ground black pepper
   to taste

Halve each chicken breast ① and trim away any fat ②. Use the butter to grease a large skillet and a piece of parchment paper or foil cut to fit the skillet exactly. Put the chicken in the pan, pour around the wine, and press the buttered paper or foil onto it ③. Cover with the lid and bring to a boil. Lower the heat so the liquid barely bubbles, and cook 8 minutes or until the chicken is opaque and firm to the touch. Transfer to a plate, reserving the cooking liquid; cover and keep warm.

Boil the cooking liquid until it is reduced to a thin film in the skillet. Pour in the cream, return to a boil, and let it bubble gently for 5 minutes. Set aside.

Heat the olive oil in another skillet and cook the pepper for a few minutes over a high heat. Pour in the cream mixture and stir thoroughly. Add salt and pepper to taste.

Arrange the chicken breasts on a platter like the spokes of a wheel. Spoon some sauce over each one and serve at once with rice pilaf.

YIELD

Serves 6

Per serving
calories 694, protein 32 g,
fat 58 g, sodium 312 mg,
carbohydrates 9 g,
potassium 619 mg

TIME

20 minutes preparation
40 minutes cooking

INGREDIENTS

6 pork loin chops
3 tablespoons butter
1 onion, thickly sliced
1 red eating apple, cored and sliced
   (skin on)
1 ½ tablespoons flour
½ cup apple juice or cider
½ cup chicken stock
Salt and freshly ground black pepper
   to taste

½ cup heavy cream
Handful of fresh parsley sprigs, finely
   chopped

Set the oven at 350 degrees. Slash the fat side of the pork chops so they don't curl during cooking ①. Melt the butter in a flameproof casserole and brown the pork chops a few at a time. Remove them from the pan, lower the heat, and cook the onion for a few minutes or until it begins to soften. Add the apple slices and sprinkle the flour into the pan ②. Cook, scraping the bottom constantly, until the flour is browned. At once pour in the apple juice or cider and the stock ③ and cook, stirring, until the sauce comes to a boil.

Replace the pork chops, turn them in the sauce, add salt and pepper to taste, cover, and cook in the preheated oven for 20 minutes, turning them over halfway through cooking.

Arrange the chops on a platter, cover with foil, and keep warm. Strain the cooking liquid into a saucepan and bring to a rolling boil. Skim the surface thoroughly, then pour in the cream and let the mixture bubble constantly for 2 minutes. Taste the sauce for seasoning, add more salt and pepper if necessary, and pour the sauce over the pork chops. Sprinkle some chopped parsley in a band down the center of the dish and serve with plain boiled rice.

YIELD

Serves 4

Per serving
calories 554, protein 59 g,
fat 32 g, sodium 411 mg,
carbohydrates 4 g,
potassium 645 mg

TIME

15 minutes preparation
25 minutes cooking

INGREDIENTS

1 carrot, cut into matchsticks
6 tablespoons butter
1 leek, trimmed, washed thoroughly,
    and thinly sliced
1 stalk celery, cut into matchsticks
Salt and freshly ground black pepper
    to taste
4 whole boneless chicken breasts

Set the oven at 400 degrees. Put the carrots into a saucepan with cold water to cover and bring to a boil. Cook steadily for 2 minutes, then drain and rinse with cold water.

Cut 4 12-inch circles from cooking parchment and use 2 tablespoons of the butter to grease the circles to within 2 inches of the edges ①.

Melt the remaining butter in a skillet and cook the carrots, leeks, and celery with plenty of salt and pepper to taste over a medium heat for 3 minutes. Set aside for a few minutes to cool.

Remove the skin from the chicken breasts ② and discard any fat pockets on the meat. Divide the breasts in half and set both halves to one side of each piece of buttered parchment. Scatter some of the vegetables on each one and fold over the other half. Crimp the edges shut by turning the outside edge over and over onto itself ③. Set the packets on a baking sheet and bake in the preheated oven for 25 minutes or until the paper is puffed and the chicken feels firm to the touch through the paper.

Transfer quickly to plates and serve at once with buttered whole potatoes.

YIELD

Serves 6

Per serving
calories 168, protein 3 g,
fat 9 g, sodium 88 mg,
carbohydrates 19 g,
potassium 619 mg

TIME

25 minutes preparation
15 minutes cooking

INGREDIENTS

2 carrots, sliced
2 potatoes, diced
2 tomatoes, cored and sliced
2 zucchini, sliced
1 onion, diced
½ pound green beans, sliced thinly
    lengthwise
Salt and freshly ground black pepper
    to taste
Pinch each of dried basil and oregano
¼ cup olive oil

Put the carrots and potatoes into a saucepan with cold water to cover and bring to a boil. Cover and cook steadily for 3 minutes or until the vegetables are partially cooked. Drain the vegetables through a strainer set over a bowl and leave the vegetables and liquid to cool.

Layer the tomatoes, zucchini, onion, green beans, carrots, and potatoes in a small flameproof casserole ①, sprinkling the layers with salt and pepper, basil, oregano, and olive oil ②.

Pour in the liquid from cooking the carrots and potatoes ③ and set the casserole over a medium-high heat. Cover and cook for 10 minutes, turning them gently halfway through cooking.

Transfer to a covered dish and pass freshly grated parmesan or romano cheese separately.

YIELD

Serves 4

Per serving
calories 805, protein 44 g,
fat 68 g, sodium 318 mg,
carbohydrates 2 g,
potassium 823 mg

TIME

10 minutes preparation
10 minutes cooking

INGREDIENTS

4 fillet steaks, cut 1½ inches thick
2 tablespoons il
Salt and freshly ground black pepper
    to taste
Small bunch of watercress for garnish

SAUCE

2 tablespoons lemon juice
3 egg yolks
Salt and freshly ground black pepper
    to taste
¾ cup unsalted butter, cut up
1 shallot, very finely chopped
1 teaspoon chopped fresh tarragon or
    chopped vinegar-preserved
    tarragon

Let the fillet steaks sit at room temperature for 20 minutes. Heat the oil in a large skillet and when it is quite hot, add the steaks with salt and pepper to taste and cook over a fairly high heat, turning them every minute until they have cooked for 6 minutes altogether (for rare steak), 8 minutes (for medium steak), and 10 minutes (for well-done steak).

Meanwhile, put the lemon juice and egg yolks in the container of a blender or food processor and add salt and pepper to taste ①. Melt the butter, turn on the machine, remove the insert cap, and drizzle in the hot butter in a slow steady stream ②. When it is all incorporated, turn off the machine, add the chopped shallots and tarragon ③, and turn the machine on for less than 5 seconds just to combine them.

Arrange a fillet steak on each plate and pour the mock Bearnaise on the side of each steak. Garnish with watercress and serve at once.

YIELD

Serves 4

Per serving
calories 506, protein 18 g,
fat 32 g, sodium 533 mg,
carbohydrates 36 g,
potassium 839 mg

TIME

15 minutes preparation
25 minutes cooking

INGREDIENTS

5 tablespoons butter
4 Idaho or Russet potatoes
3 tablespoons flour
2 teaspoons dry mustard
1¾ cups milk
Salt and freshly ground black pepper
　to taste
1½ cups grated cheddar cheese

Set the oven at 400 degrees. Use 2 tablespoons of the butter to grease 4 individual shallow baking dishes or gratin dishes.

Peel the potatoes and cut into thin slices. Cut across several slices at once to make matchstick pieces ①. Pile into a saucepan with cold water to cover, bring to a boil, and cook 2 minutes or until potatoes are almost tender.

Drain and shake to remove excess moisture. Divide between the 4 buttered dishes and set aside.

Melt the remaining butter in a saucepan and stir in the flour until smooth ②. Cook, whisking constantly for 1 minute. Gradually whisk in the mustard and milk ③ and stir constantly until the mixture comes to a boil. Lower the heat and let the sauce simmer for 2 minutes. Add salt and pepper to taste and pour the sauce over the potatoes. Sprinkle the cheese on top and bake the potatoes for 20 to 25 minutes or until they are crisp and brown. Serve at once.

YIELD

Serves 6

Per serving
calories 337, protein 5 g,
fat 19 g, sodium 164 mg,
carbohydrates 37 g,
potassium 257 mg

TIME

20 minutes preparation
30 minutes chilling
10 minutes cooking

INGREDIENTS

4 large Granny Smith or other tart
   eating apples
6 tablespoons butter
¼ cup sugar

SAUCE

2 cups milk
5 egg yolks
¼ cup sugar
1 teaspoon vanilla extract
Extra sugar for sprinkling

For the sauce, scald the milk in a heavy-bottomed saucepan. Blend the yolks and sugar thoroughly in a bowl with a wooden spoon and gradually stir in the hot milk. Return the mixture to the saucepan and stir over low heat until it thickens to the consistency of heavy cream. Do not boil or it will curdle.

At once strain the mixture into a bowl ① and stir in the vanilla. Sprinkle the top with a very light coating of sugar and refrigerate the sauce for 30 minutes or until cold.

Pare the apples, quarter them, and remove the stems and cores. Halve the quarters to make 32 apple wedges ②. Melt the butter in a large skillet and when it is foaming, add the apple wedges. Cook over a high heat for half a minute, then turn them over and sprinkle with the sugar. Cook another few minutes or until the sugar begins to caramelize ③, then remove the pan from the heat.

Coat 6 dessert plates with some of the custard sauce and arrange 5 or 6 apple wedges, like the spokes of a wheel, on the sauce. Serve at once.

26

YIELD

Serves 6

Per serving
calories 306, protein 2 g,
fat 25 g, sodium 27 mg,
carbohydrates 18 g,
potassium 171 mg

TIME

15 minutes preparation
30 minutes chilling

INGREDIENTS

1 pint fresh raspberries or 1 box
   (10 ounces) frozen raspberries in
   syrup, thawed
Grated rind of 1 orange
2 tablespoons confectioners' sugar
   (for fresh raspberries)
1 tablespoon Grand Marnier or other
   orange liqueur
1 cup heavy cream

4 chewy macaroons, broken into tiny
   pieces
½ cup heavy cream, stiffly whipped,
   for decoration

If using fresh raspberries, reserve 6 of them for the garnish. Put the remaining berries on a plate with the orange rind and confectioners' sugar. If using frozen raspberries, drain them in a sieve set over a bowl. Pile the berries onto a plate with the orange rind.

In both cases, mash the berries with a fork ①, adding orange liqueur to them. Add 2 tablespoons of the syrup to the frozen berries.

Whip the cream until it holds stiff peaks and fold in the berry mixture with the crushed macaroons, just until they are mixed ②.

Divide the mixture among 6 stemmed glasses and use a pastry bag and star tip to pipe a rosette on the top of each glass ③. Use the reserved 6 fresh raspberries, if available, to garnish the rosettes. Refrigerate for 30 minutes before serving with additional macaroons or crisp cookies.

27

YIELD

Serves 4

Per serving
calories 403, protein 3 g,
fat 26 g, sodium 65 mg,
carbohydrates 40 g,
potassium 111 mg

TIME

15 minutes preparation
15 minutes chilling
12 minutes cooking

INGREDIENTS

1 cup flour
Pinch of salt
½ cup unsalted butter, well chilled
   but cut up
2 tablespoons ice water

FILLING

2 northern spy or golden delicious
   apples
1 tablespoon butter
2 tablespoons sugar

Place the flour and salt in a food processor and add the cut-up butter. Turn the processor quickly on-off several times until the butter is in tiny pieces. Turn the processor off, add the ice water, and process just until the mixture is damp, not formed together as a dough. Remove it from the processor and place it on a lightly floured board. Knead the dough lightly with the heel of your hand until it comes together smoothly ①. Wrap in foil and refrigerate 15 minutes.

Set the oven at 550 degrees or your highest setting other than "broil." Set a baking sheet on the bottom-most rack of the oven.

For the filling, pare the apples, halve them, and remove the seeds and stem with the point of a knife. Then set the cut sides down on a board and make slices perpendicular to the core as thinly as possible ②. Set aside.

Roll out the pastry on a lightly floured board and when it is as thin as you can make it, use it to line an 11-inch fluted tart pan, cutting it off at the top edge so the pastry sinks below the fluted rim ③. Prick the pastry all over. Lay the apples on the tart in concentric circles. Dot them with the butter and sprinkle with sugar.

Set the tart on the hot baking heet and bake it for about 5 minutes, or until the sugar begins to caramelize. Transfer the tart to the top of the oven and continue cooking another 8 minutes or until the edges of the pastry are browned. Remove from the oven, leave to cool to lukewarm, and serve cut into fourths with a large dollop of whipped cream on each wedge.

28

YIELD

Serves 4

Per serving
calories 225, protein 1 g,
fat 17 g, sodium 18 mg,
carbohydrates 18 g,
potassium 223 mg

TIME

15 minutes preparation
1 hour chilling

INGREDIENTS

1½ pints fresh strawberries
3 tablespoons sugar
¾ cup heavy cream

Reserve 8 perfect-looking berries and set aside for the garnish. Stem the remaining berries and mash them on a deep plate with a fork ①, sprinkling them with sugar. Leave for a few minutes.

In a chilled bowl with chilled beaters, beat the cream until it holds stiff peaks ②. Fold in the fruit pulp and liquid until incorporated. Transfer to tall stemmed glasses and refrigerate for 1 hour.

Without removing the stems from the reserved strawberries make 4 or 5 lengthwise slices from the tip almost to the stem, leaving the berry completely intact at the stem end ③. With your fingers fan these slices and arrange 2 strawberry "fans" on each glass. Serve at once with crisp cookies.

SAFFRON FISH CHOWDER

YIELD

Serves 6

Per serving
calories 500, protein 47 g,
fat 20 g, sodium 1348 mg,
carbohydrates 18 g,
potassium 1269 mg

TIME

20 minutes preparation
15 minutes cooking

INGREDIENTS

1 heaping teaspoon saffron threads
1/4 teaspoon sugar
6 cups bottled clam juice
2 cups dry white wine
6 tablespoons butter
4 medium carrots, halved lengthwise
   and sliced
2 medium onions, coarsely chopped

Salt and freshly ground black pepper
   to taste
2 cloves garlic, crushed
3 pounds firm-fleshed boneless white
   fish (cod, haddock, cusk, tilefish)
1/2 cup heavy cream
Bunch of fresh parsley, finely chopped

Work the saffron and sugar in a small bowl with the back of a spoon until they form a fine powder. Set aside. Combine the clam juice and wine in a saucepan and bring to a boil. Boil to reduce mixture to 6 cups.

Melt the butter in a large flameproof casserole and cook the carrots and onions over a low heat for 5 minutes or until they are soft but not browned. Add the salt, pepper, garlic, saffron, and clam juice mixture and bring to a boil. Simmer 2 minutes.

Cut the fish into 2-inch chunks and very carefully set the fish in the hot liquid. Spoon some of the liquid at the sides onto the fish and cover the top. Lower the heat and cook for 2 minutes. Carefully turn the fish over in the liquid, recover pan, and remove from heat. Let sit for 5 minutes or until the fish is firm and opaque.

Add the cream to the chowder, return the liquid to a boil, and carefully spoon some of the liquid on the sides onto the fish to mix in the cream. Taste for seasoning, add more salt and pepper if necessary, and serve at once, sprinkling each bowl with some chopped parsley.

CORN, HAM, AND POTATO CHOWDER

YIELD

Serves 4

Per serving
calories 817, protein 37 g,
fat 56 g, sodium 1176 mg,
carbohydrates 44 g,
potassium 1211 mg

TIME

15 minutes preparation
10 minutes cooking

INGREDIENTS

4 ears of cooked or uncooked fresh
   corn
4 tablespoons butter
2 medium onions, chopped
2 medium potatoes, peeled and diced
1 pound thickly sliced Virginia or other
   flavorful ham, diced
3–4 cups milk
1 cup light cream

Salt and freshly ground black pepper
   to taste
1 green pepper, cored and diced
Handful of parsley sprigs, finely
   chopped

Use a small, sharp knife to scrape the corn from the cob. Set aside. Melt butter in a large saucepan and cook onions until they are soft but not brown. Add potatoes and stir until they begin to stick to the pan.

Add the ham, most of the milk, the cream, and salt and pepper to taste. Bring to a boil, lower the heat quickly (take care that milk does not bubble over), and cook soup for 5 minutes so liquid barely bubbles. Add green pepper, taste for seasoning, and continue cooking for 3 minutes or until potatoes are tender. Taste the soup for seasoning, stir in parsley, and add enough of the remaining milk to make the consistency you prefer. Serve at once with corn muffins or cornbread.

ORANGE CREAMS

YIELD

Serves 4

Per serving
calories 366, protein 5 g,
fat 19 g, sodium 25 mg,
carbohydrates 40 g,
potassium 252 mg

TIME

5 minutes preparation
2 hours chilling
10 minutes cooking

INGREDIENTS

6 egg yolks
1/2 cup sugar
Grated rind and strained juice of
    2 large juice oranges
2 tablespoons Grand Marnier or other
    orange liqueur
1/2 cup heavy cream, stiffly whipped
4 very thin strips of orange rind

In a small, heavy-bottomed saucepan or in the top of a double boiler, combine the egg yolks, sugar, orange rind, juice, and Grand Marnier. Whisk the mixture until it is combined, then set it over low heat or over hot but not boiling water and cook, stirring constantly, just until the mixture thickens enough to hold its shape. Do not boil or it will curdle.

Set the saucepan in a roasting pan filled with ice and stir the custard with a rubber spatula until it has cooled completely. Replace the ice when necessary.

Pour the custard into 4 coupe or stemmed glasses and cover each with plastic wrap. Refrigerate for 2 hours or until they are quite cold. Garnish with whipped cream and twist the orange strips to decorate the cream.

APRICOT BREAD PUDDING

YIELD

Serves 6

Per serving
calories 598, protein 15 g,
fat 30 g, sodium 586 mg,
carbohydrates 66 g,
potassium 523 mg

TIME

10 minutes preparation
1 hour cooking

INGREDIENTS

1 cup dried apricots
1/4 cup butter, at room temperature
12 thin slices French bread
Grated rind of 1 lemon
1/3 cup sugar
6 eggs, lightly beaten
2 cups light cream

Set the oven at 350 degrees. Lightly butter a 2-quart baking dish. Cover the apricots with boiling water and let them sit for 5 minutes to "plump" slightly. Drain and quarter them; set aside.

Butter the French bread on one side and lay some slices, buttered side up, in the baking dish. Sprinkle with apricots, lemon rind, and sugar. Make another layer of bread, fruit, and sugar (reserving 2 tablespoons of sugar for the top), ending with a layer of bread arranged in a neat overlapping pattern.

Mix the eggs and cream and pour them into the dish at the side. Sprinkle the top with the remaining 2 tablespoons of sugar and set the dish in a roasting pan.

Pour in enough boiling water to come halfway up the sides of the baking dish, and bake the pudding for 1 hour or until a knife inserted into the custard comes out clean. Remove the baking dish from the roasting pan and let the pudding cool slightly before serving.

INDEX

The following numbers refer to recipe numbers, not page numbers.